CONTENTS

WHAT CAN ASTROLOGY
do for me?

Astrology is a powerful tool for self-awareness. The idea that we are all connected—that the shifting energies of the Sun, Moon, and planets above affect us here on Earth—is an ancient and philosophical belief. Astrology isn't fortune-telling—it can't predict your future and it doesn't deal in absolutes. It simply says that you are part of the universe around you, and by studying the stars, it's possible to learn more about yourself.

Why is this so important? Because the better understanding you have of your own inner makeup—your skills, your talents, your needs, and your fears—the more insight you gain into why you act the way you do. And this gives you choices, empowering you to make changes and to build on your strengths. It makes it easier to feel confident and to accept yourself, quirks and all.

There are countless daily horoscopes in newspapers, magazines, and online. But this book looks at more than just your star sign, which is only a small part of your personality picture. It helps you to find your Rising sign, which was appearing over the Eastern horizon at the time of your birth, and has a lot to tell you about the way others see you. You can also work out your Moon sign, which reveals the real you deep down inside, giving you the chance to get to grips with your innermost emotions, desires, fears, and obsessions.

With a clearer picture of who you are, life becomes less complicated. Instead of trying to live up to others' expectations and being someone you're not, you can work instead on becoming the best version of yourself possible—someone who understands their talents and needs, who is perfectly unique, and is happy.

What is
ASTROLOGY?

The stars and planets have always inspired a sense of wonder. The ancient peoples of Babylonia, Persia, Egypt, Greece, and India were all fascinated by the cycles of the Moon, the rising and setting of the Sun, the position of the constellations, and what it all meant. As these civilizations developed, they connected what they saw in the sky with the people and events on Earth, and astrology was born.

In ancient times, astrology was used to help monarchs rule. Kings and emperors would employ astrologers to predict the weather, speak to the gods, and help manage the country.

Modern astrology has evolved to help ordinary people like you and me understand ourselves better—how we behave, how we feel about each other, and how we can make the best of who we are.

THE SIGNS OF THE ZODIAC

Today we know that the planets revolve around the Sun, but astrology is based on how we see the solar system from here on Earth. The Zodiac is a group of 12 constellations that, from our viewpoint, seem to rotate around Earth over the course of a year, like a huge wheel. These constellations are named for the animals and objects that our ancestors thought they looked most like—the ram, the lion, the scorpion, and so on. Your Sun sign tells you which of the constellations the Sun was moving through on the day you were born. The signs have a natural order that never varies, beginning with Aries. The dates given on the right change slightly from year to year for the same reasons we have a leap year—each of our days is slightly longer than 24 hours. If you were born at the beginning or end of a sign, called "the cusp," it's worth checking your Sun sign online to be sure.

ARIES	LIBRA
March 21–April 20	September 23–October 22
TAURUS	SCORPIO
April 21–May 21	October 23–November 21
GEMINI	SAGITTARIUS
May 22–June 21	November 22–December 21
CANCER	CAPRICORN
June 22–July 22	December 22–January 20
LEO	AQUARIUS
July 23–August 23	January 21–February 19
VIRGO	PISCES
August 24–September 22	February 20–March 20

THE FOUR ELEMENTS

Each Sun sign is associated with one of four elements—
Fire, Earth, Air, and Water.

FIRE

Aries, Leo, Sagittarius
Fire signs are passionate, dynamic, and temperamental.
They mix well with: Fire and Air types

EARTH

Taurus, Virgo, Capricorn
Earth signs are practical, cautious, and reliable.
They mix well with: Water and Earth types

AIR

Gemini, Libra, Aquarius
Air signs are quick, curious, and adventurous.
They mix well with: Air and Fire types

WATER

Cancer, Scorpio, Pisces
Water signs are sensitive, emotional, and kind.
They mix well with: Earth and Water types

THE PLANETS

Astrology looks at the positions of the stars and planets at the time and place of your birth. The Sun and Moon aren't technically planets, but they're referred to that way by astrologers for ease of use. The Sun is a great place to start—it's the most important object in the solar system. Your Sun sign describes the essence of your identity and says a great deal about your potential—the person you might become.

The position the Moon held in the sky at the time of your birth has a strong influence, too. It describes your emotions—how you feel deep inside. It can give you a better understanding of what you need to feel loved and cared for.

And there's also your Rising sign. This is the sign of the Zodiac that was appearing over the Eastern horizon at the time of your birth. It tells you more about how you interact with the world around you, especially to new situations. It's the filter through which you perceive the world and the impression you give to others on first meeting. Which means it's also how others often see you.

The positions of the other planets—Venus, Mercury, Mars, etc.—in your birth chart all have their own effect. But these three taken together—Sun, Moon, and Rising sign—will give you a deeper understanding of who you are and what you could become, your strengths and weaknesses, your real self.

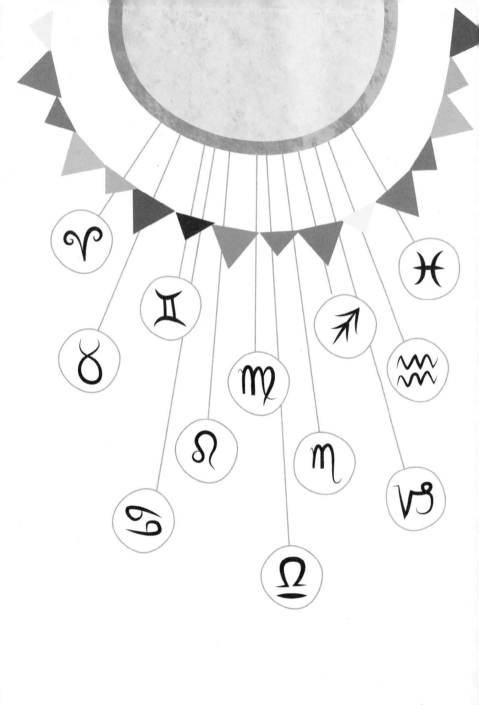

Your SUN sign

PISCES

SYMBOL
The Fishes

ELEMENT
Water

RULING PLANET
Neptune

BIRTHSTONE
Aquamarine

COLOR
Sea green

BODY PART
Feet

DAY OF THE WEEK
Thursday

FLOWER
Water Lily

CHARACTER TRAITS
Dreamy, sensitive, compassionate

KEY PHRASE
"I believe"

YOUR SUN SIGN

When people talk about astrology and ask about your star sign, they're referring to your Sun sign. It tells you which of the 12 constellations of the Zodiac the Sun was moving through on the day you were born. This makes it easy to work out, which is one of the reasons for its popularity. If you'd like to know the Sun sign of a friend or family member, the table on page 7 shows which days the Sun occupies each of the signs over the course of a year.

The Sun is the heart of your chart—it's the essence of who you are and symbolizes the potential of what you can achieve. It's important to remember, though, that it is only a part of the whole picture when it comes to astrology. It's a wonderful starting point, but there are many other layers encasing your core identity, all of which affect the inner you.

ALL ABOUT YOU

Born with the Sun in Pisces, you have the potential to help others connect to their spiritual side. Water symbolizes emotions, and Pisces—represented by two fish swimming in different directions—is the most sensitive of the Zodiac signs. This means you prefer to seek out super-kind friends: anyone with a harsher edge might upset your finely tuned heart.

You have a rich imagination (Water is also closely linked to creativity), and you often drift off into your own dream world. Your friends are used to it and may even find it funny, but it's probably a different story with your teachers, who just don't understand how fabulous your imaginary world is.

Those lucky enough to be on your friendship list quickly find out what a generous, compassionate, and caring friend you are, and this can make you the go-to person in a crisis. Just remember not to get so caught up in the worries of others you forget about what you want. Being so sensitive, it's worth setting boundaries, or others may take advantage.

Likes

Arts and crafts
To be loved
Privacy
Hugs
Music

Dislikes

Being criticized
Animal cruelty
Confrontation

HOW TO BRING OUT YOUR BEST

You love to go with the flow. But here's the thing: you can sometimes feel directionless if you don't keep an eye on things. You can be distracted easily— when something more enticing appears on the horizon, you're drawn toward it.

You always see the best in everyone and can be blind to being manipulated by others, but you feel happiest when you're helping people, especially with their emotions. It takes strength and courage to accept others for who they are, and you have a hidden resilience that allows you to take on the feelings of those around you and help them be at peace with themselves. Learning to stay afloat when the world around you is turbulent and stormy is one of your life challenges.

The spiritual side of life interests you, so you will increasingly find yourself drawn to explore this. Your friends might tease you, but that strong intuition of yours tells you when you're following the right path.

Strengths

Artistic
Intuitive
Mystical
Imaginative
Accepting
Thoughtful
Selfless

Weaknesses

Overly trusting
Unrealistic
Moody

SECRET FEARS

You spend too much time in fantasyland now and then, and when reality does come a-knocking, you're brought back down to earth with a bump.

You're wonderful at supporting others but can be scared to admit when you need help yourself. Burying your feelings can just make them more difficult to deal with when they eventually pop back up—which they will.

You're hugely creative, but getting motivated to put some of your magical ideas into motion can prove tricky, and you worry others might see this as a sign of laziness. Don't sweat it—they'll soon understand it's simply the sign of a creative genius at work!

Most likely to . . .

Go with the flow

Forgive and forget

See a ghost

Daydream

Cry at a movie

Try to fit in

Comfort a friend

Your RISING sign

YOUR RISING SIGN

Your Rising sign, also known as your Ascendant, is the sign that was rising over the Eastern horizon (the place where the Sun rises each day) when you were born. It describes how you see the world and the people around you and how they see you—the first impression that you give and receive, the image you project, and the initial reaction you might have to a new situation. A person with Leo Rising, for example, may strike you as warm and engaging, whereas Pisces Rising is more sensitive and possibly shy. Because the Ascendant is determined by the exact time and place you were born, it is the most personal point in your chart. Many astrologers believe this makes it just as important as your Sun sign.

HOW TO FIND YOUR ASCENDANT

This is where it gets a bit tricky. There's a reason that popular astrology only deals with your Sun sign—your Rising sign can be more difficult to work out. But don't be put off. If you know your Sun sign and your time of birth, you can use the table on the right to give you a good idea. To be totally accurate you do need to take into account factors like time zone and daylight savings, and there are plenty of free online calculators that will do just that.

YOUR SUN SIGN	6:00 AM to 8:00 AM	8:00 AM to 10:00 AM	10:00 AM to 12:00 PM	12:00 PM to 2:00 PM	2:00 PM to 4:00 PM	4:00 PM to 6:00 PM	6:00 PM to 8:00 PM	8:00 PM to 10:00 PM	10:00 PM to 12:00 AM	12:00 AM to 2:00 AM	2:00 AM to 4:00 AM	4:00 AM to 6:00 AM
ARIES	Taurus	Gemini	Cancer	Leo	Virgo	Libra	Scorpio	Sagittarius	Capricorn	Aquarius	Pisces	Aries
TAURUS	Gemini	Cancer	Leo	Virgo	Libra	Scorpio	Sagittarius	Capricorn	Aquarius	Pisces	Aries	Taurus
GEMINI	Cancer	Leo	Virgo	Libra	Scorpio	Sagittarius	Capricorn	Aquarius	Pisces	Aries	Taurus	Gemini
CANCER	Leo	Virgo	Libra	Scorpio	Sagittarius	Capricorn	Aquarius	Pisces	Aries	Taurus	Gemini	Cancer
LEO	Virgo	Libra	Scorpio	Sagittarius	Capricorn	Aquarius	Pisces	Aries	Taurus	Gemini	Cancer	Leo
VIRGO	Libra	Scorpio	Sagittarius	Capricorn	Aquarius	Pisces	Aries	Taurus	Gemini	Cancer	Leo	Virgo
LIBRA	Scorpio	Sagittarius	Capricorn	Aquarius	Pisces	Aries	Taurus	Gemini	Cancer	Leo	Virgo	Libra
SCORPIO	Sagittarius	Capricorn	Aquarius	Pisces	Aries	Taurus	Gemini	Cancer	Leo	Virgo	Libra	Scorpio
SAGITTARIUS	Capricorn	Aquarius	Pisces	Aries	Taurus	Gemini	Cancer	Leo	Virgo	Libra	Scorpio	Sagittarius
CAPRICORN	Aquarius	Pisces	Aries	Taurus	Gemini	Cancer	Leo	Virgo	Libra	Scorpio	Sagittarius	Capricorn
AQUARIUS	Pisces	Aries	Taurus	Gemini	Cancer	Leo	Virgo	Libra	Scorpio	Sagittarius	Capricorn	Aquarius
PISCES	Aries	Taurus	Gemini	Cancer	Leo	Virgo	Libra	Scorpio	Sagittarius	Capricorn	Aquarius	Pisces

WHAT YOUR RISING SIGN SAYS ABOUT YOU

Once you have figured out your Ascendant, you are ready to discover more about how you see the world, and how it sees you.

ARIES RISING

A dash of fiery Aries in Pisces heats things up a little. You impress your teachers and friends alike with your impressive energy reserves. Unlike others, you don't struggle to get out of bed in the morning: you spring up, ready to take on the day. However, while you may feel invincible, it's also important to regularly recharge. Relaxing sports like swimming and yoga will benefit you. Your ability to fire on all cylinders will continue into adulthood, so vocations that demand total focus—such as medicine—might be worth exploring.

TAURUS RISING

Taurus brings a strong-willed quality to the Pisces party. You can be something of a dreamer, but this combination gives you the focus and determination to get those school assignments in on time or to train for a sporting event. Any monthly allowance your parents give you is likely to end up being spent on gifts for your friends—you are generous and love to spoil them when you can. In the workplace, you're likely to attract powerful people like a magnet. The best bit? They'll be only too happy to give you a leg-up in your chosen profession.

GEMINI RISING

Gemini brings a deep curiosity about the world. Whether it's astronomy, history, or fashion, nothing is off the table when it comes to subjects that interest you. You're eager to absorb as much information as quickly as you can. However, your friends might sometimes feel like you're not giving them your full attention because you're always thinking of the next thing on your long to-do list. Try to be in the moment more often and stop yourself from racing ahead mentally.

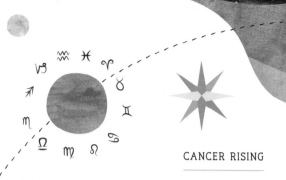

CANCER RISING

With two Water signs flowing into each other, a gentle heart is often the result. You're happy when your bestie tells you everything because you show your love by nurturing people. You're awesome at tricking others, too. Not in a nasty way, but in an "I'm-organizing-a-secret-party-for-you-that-you-know-zilch-about" kind of way. That ability, backed up with quite an industrious nature, could mean that you are the hottest event organizer in town in later life.

LEO RISING

This is a match made in drama heaven. Your artistic Pisces sensibility can find expression through Leo's theatrical nature. If anyone is going to make a song and dance about anything, it's you—but if you can harness this energy, you will be the one to watch in school stage productions. In adulthood, you'll naturally be drawn to the theater, but having a backup plan waiting in the wings for the leaner times is always a good idea.

VIRGO RISING

With Virgo's practicality on board, those born with this combination just love to come to the rescue. You have a strong empathetic streak, so you will usually have a line of friends waiting in line to cry on your shoulder. But while you're busy doing things for other people, it allows you to be distracted from what's going on in your own life. Perhaps you can carve out a couple of days a week where you don't answer an SOS call from a loved one? It may be hard to begin with, but it will help you to replenish your own emotional reserves.

LIBRA RISING

A Pisces/Libra blend brings with it a lovely sense of harmony and calmness, both in your life and for those you hold closest. During exam time, for example, your chilled energy will rub off on your friends, who may be in panic mode. Bear in mind that your desire to keep the peace can come with a personal cost if you're not careful. It's key not to lose your sense of self by being too obliging.

SCORPIO RISING

It's a wonder that those born under this pairing don't pop out with a paintbrush in their hand! Ideas and images leap from your vivid imagination, and you'll probably be the star student in your high school art class. You can be a little impetuous—rushing headlong into something and thinking about the consequences later—and learning to think a situation through some more will be one of your life challenges. If you're not wowing the art world when you enter adulthood, you may be drawn to deadline-driven jobs because you seem to respond so well to pressure.

SAGITTARIUS RISING

If you're lucky enough to have this pairing, you'll be known for your happy smile, which you wear pretty much 24/7. In your school yearbook, you may well be named "Most Popular" several years running. But you're happy to let others bask in your glow because of your kind heart. As you make your way in the world of work, watch out for others who might take advantage of your rosy view of life. Listen to your intuition: your strong inner compass will keep you on track.

CAPRICORN RISING

Capricorn's down-to-earth energy anchors the Pisces' tendency to let their feelings run away with them. You are quite a sensible soul and love to win the approval of your friends and teachers. Not much throws you into a spin, and you seem to understand the ways of the world pretty quickly; your classmates have you down as the wise old owl! You can also put this wisdom to good use in your adult life: a career involving psychology could have your name all over it.

AQUARIUS RISING

An Aquarius/Pisces combination creates an awesome imagination. You have a highly original approach to everything and see the world through a magical lens. At school, your art projects will stand out from those of your classmates, but you may struggle a little with more mundane subjects. Don't get down-hearted: we all have different strengths. If you decide to run with your creative side later in life, you could become one-to-watch on the art scene.

PISCES RISING

High sensitivity is commonplace with a double helping of Pisces. A friend may come to you when they're feeling blue, and because of your empathy—the ability to feel someone else's emotions—you can end up even bluer. At times it may even be difficult to tell if you are feeling your own emotions or someone else's. If you do find yourself overwhelmed or exhausted, or absorbing the stress and negativity of others, that's your body telling you it's time to step away and recharge. Mindful coloring or breathing exercises can be great escapes.

Your MOON sign

YOUR MOON SIGN

The Moon rules your emotions and your inner moods, telling you what you need to feel safe, comfortable, and loved. Knowing your Moon sign should give you a more complete picture of your unique self, helping you to express needs you might be struggling to understand. Suppose your Sun sign is Aries but being first has never been important to you—a Moon in Virgo may be telling you to hang back and fade into the background. Or you might have the Sun in home-loving Cancer but feel an urge to get out there and see the world. Perhaps that's because your Moon is in freedom-loving Sagittarius.

HOW TO FIND YOUR MOON SIGN

Just like your Rising sign, finding your Moon sign is more complicated than finding your Sun sign. That's because the Moon seems to move so quickly, taking just about a month to pass through all of the constellations. Thankfully, the tables on the right and on the next page make finding it a simple process.

First, find your year of birth. Then locate your birth month at the top of the table. Find your date of birth in the column below it, and this will give you your Moon sign. If your date of birth isn't listed, the one before it is your Moon sign.

For example, suppose your date of birth is March 4, 1995. The date before this is March 2, for which the Moon sign is Aries. This would mean your Moon sign is Aries.

JAN	FEB	MAR	APR	MAY	JUN	JUL	AUG	SEP	OCT	NOV	DEC

BORN IN THE YEAR 1995

JAN	FEB	MAR	APR	MAY	JUN	JUL	AUG	SEP	OCT	NOV	DEC
2 Aqu	1 Pis	2 Ari	1 Tau	1 Gem	2 Leo	2 Vir	3 Sco	1 Sag	2 Aqu	1 Pis	3 Tau
4 Pis	3 Ari	5 Tau	3 Gem	3 Can	5 Vir	4 Lib	5 Sag	3 Cap	5 Pis	3 Ari	5 Gem
7 Ari	5 Tau	7 Gem	6 Can	6 Leo	7 Lib	6 Sco	7 Cap	5 Aqu	7 Ari	5 Tau	8 Can
9 Tau	8 Gem	10 Can	9 Leo	8 Vir	9 Sco	8 Sag	9 Aqu	7 Pis	9 Tau	8 Gem	10 Leo
12 Gem	10 Can	12 Leo	11 Vir	10 Lib	11 Sag	10 Cap	11 Pis	9 Ari	12 Gem	10 Can	13 Vir
14 Can	13 Leo	14 Vir	13 Lib	13 Sco	13 Cap	12 Aqu	13 Ari	12 Tau	14 Can	13 Leo	15 Lib
16 Leo	15 Vir	17 Lib	15 Sco	15 Sag	15 Aqu	14 Pis	15 Tau	14 Gem	17 Leo	15 Vir	17 Sco
19 Vir	17 Lib	19 Sco	17 Sag	17 Cap	17 Pis	17 Ari	18 Gem	17 Can	19 Vir	18 Lib	19 Sag
21 Lib	19 Sco	21 Sag	19 Cap	19 Aqu	19 Ari	19 Tau	20 Can	19 Leo	21 Lib	20 Sco	21 Cap
23 Sco	22 Sag	23 Cap	21 Aqu	21 Pis	22 Tau	22 Gem	23 Leo	22 Vir	23 Sco	22 Sag	23 Aqu
25 Sag	24 Cap	25 Aqu	24 Pis	23 Ari	24 Gem	24 Can	25 Vir	24 Lib	26 Sag	24 Cap	25 Pis
27 Cap	26 Aqu	27 Pis	26 Ari	26 Tau	27 Can	27 Leo	28 Lib	26 Sco	28 Cap	26 Aqu	28 Ari
30 Aqu	28 Pis	30 Ari	28 Tau	28 Gem	29 Leo	29 Vir	30 Sco	28 Sag	30 Aqu	28 Pis	30 Tau
				31 Can		31 Lib		30 Cap		30 Ari	

BORN IN THE YEAR 1996

JAN	FEB	MAR	APR	MAY	JUN	JUL	AUG	SEP	OCT	NOV	DEC
1 Gem	3 Leo	1 Leo	2 Lib	2 Sco	2 Cap	2 Aqu	2 Ari	1 Tau	3 Can	2 Leo	2 Vir
4 Can	5 Vir	3 Vir	4 Sco	4 Sag	4 Aqu	4 Pis	4 Tau	3 Gem	5 Leo	4 Vir	4 Lib
6 Leo	8 Lib	6 Lib	7 Sag	6 Cap	6 Pis	6 Ari	7 Gem	6 Can	8 Vir	7 Lib	6 Sco
9 Vir	10 Sco	8 Sco	9 Cap	8 Aqu	9 Ari	8 Tau	9 Can	8 Leo	10 Lib	9 Sco	9 Sag
11 Lib	12 Sag	10 Sag	11 Aqu	10 Pis	11 Tau	11 Gem	12 Leo	11 Vir	13 Sco	11 Sag	11 Cap
14 Sco	14 Cap	13 Cap	13 Pis	12 Ari	13 Gem	13 Can	14 Vir	13 Lib	15 Sag	13 Cap	13 Aqu
16 Sag	16 Aqu	15 Aqu	15 Ari	15 Tau	16 Can	16 Leo	17 Lib	15 Sco	17 Cap	16 Aqu	15 Pis
18 Cap	18 Pis	17 Pis	17 Tau	17 Gem	18 Leo	18 Vir	19 Sco	18 Sag	19 Aqu	18 Pis	17 Ari
20 Aqu	20 Ari	19 Ari	20 Gem	19 Can	21 Vir	21 Lib	21 Sag	20 Cap	21 Pis	20 Ari	19 Tau
22 Pis	23 Tau	21 Tau	22 Can	22 Leo	23 Lib	23 Sco	24 Cap	22 Aqu	23 Ari	22 Tau	22 Gem
24 Ari	25 Gem	23 Gem	25 Leo	25 Vir	26 Sco	25 Sag	26 Aqu	24 Pis	26 Tau	24 Gem	24 Can
26 Tau	27 Can	26 Can	27 Vir	27 Lib	28 Sag	27 Cap	28 Pis	26 Ari	28 Gem	27 Can	26 Leo
29 Gem		28 Leo	30 Lib	29 Sco	30 Cap	29 Aqu	30 Ari	28 Tau	30 Can	29 Leo	29 Vir
31 Can		31 Vir		31 Sag		31 Pis		30 Gem			31 Lib

BORN IN THE YEAR 1997

JAN	FEB	MAR	APR	MAY	JUN	JUL	AUG	SEP	OCT	NOV	DEC
3 Sco	1 Sag	1 Sag	1 Aqu	1 Pis	1 Tau	1 Gem	2 Leo	3 Lib	3 Sco	1 Sag	1 Cap
5 Sag	4 Cap	3 Cap	4 Pis	3 Ari	4 Gem	3 Can	4 Vir	6 Sco	5 Sag	4 Cap	3 Aqu
7 Cap	6 Aqu	5 Aqu	6 Ari	5 Tau	6 Can	5 Leo	7 Lib	8 Sag	8 Cap	6 Aqu	5 Pis
9 Aqu	8 Pis	7 Pis	8 Tau	7 Gem	8 Leo	8 Vir	9 Sco	10 Cap	10 Aqu	8 Pis	8 Ari
11 Pis	10 Ari	9 Ari	10 Gem	9 Can	11 Vir	10 Lib	12 Sag	12 Aqu	12 Pis	10 Ari	10 Tau
13 Ari	12 Tau	11 Tau	12 Can	12 Leo	13 Lib	13 Sco	14 Cap	15 Pis	14 Ari	12 Tau	12 Gem
15 Tau	14 Gem	13 Gem	14 Leo	14 Vir	16 Sco	15 Sag	16 Aqu	17 Ari	16 Tau	14 Gem	14 Can
18 Gem	16 Can	16 Can	17 Vir	17 Lib	18 Sag	18 Cap	18 Pis	19 Tau	18 Gem	17 Can	16 Leo
20 Can	19 Leo	18 Leo	19 Lib	19 Sco	20 Cap	20 Aqu	20 Ari	21 Gem	20 Can	19 Leo	19 Vir
23 Leo	21 Vir	21 Vir	22 Sco	22 Sag	22 Aqu	22 Pis	22 Tau	23 Can	23 Leo	21 Vir	21 Lib
25 Vir	24 Lib	23 Lib	24 Sag	24 Cap	24 Pis	24 Ari	24 Gem	25 Leo	25 Vir	24 Lib	24 Sco
28 Lib	26 Sco	26 Sco	27 Cap	26 Aqu	26 Ari	26 Tau	27 Can	28 Vir	28 Lib	26 Sco	26 Sag
30 Sco		28 Sag	29 Aqu	28 Pis	29 Tau	28 Gem	29 Leo	30 Lib	30 Sco	29 Sag	28 Cap
		30 Cap		30 Ari		30 Can	31 Vir				31 Aqu

BORN IN THE YEAR 1998

JAN	FEB	MAR	APR	MAY	JUN	JUL	AUG	SEP	OCT	NOV	DEC
2 Pis	2 Tau	2 Tau	2 Can	2 Leo	3 Lib	3 Sco	2 Sag	3 Aqu	2 Pis	1 Ari	2 Gem
4 Ari	4 Gem	4 Gem	4 Leo	4 Vir	5 Sco	5 Sag	4 Cap	5 Pis	4 Ari	3 Tau	4 Can
6 Tau	7 Can	6 Can	7 Vir	7 Lib	8 Sag	8 Cap	6 Aqu	7 Ari	6 Tau	5 Gem	6 Leo
8 Gem	9 Leo	8 Leo	9 Lib	9 Sco	10 Cap	10 Aqu	8 Pis	9 Tau	8 Gem	7 Can	9 Vir
10 Can	11 Vir	11 Vir	12 Sco	12 Sag	13 Aqu	12 Pis	11 Ari	11 Gem	10 Can	9 Leo	11 Lib
13 Leo	14 Lib	13 Lib	14 Sag	14 Cap	15 Pis	14 Ari	13 Tau	13 Can	13 Leo	11 Vir	14 Sco
15 Vir	16 Sco	16 Sco	17 Cap	16 Aqu	17 Ari	16 Tau	15 Gem	15 Leo	15 Vir	14 Lib	16 Sag
18 Lib	19 Sag	18 Sag	19 Aqu	19 Pis	19 Tau	18 Gem	17 Can	18 Vir	17 Lib	16 Sco	19 Cap
20 Sco	21 Cap	21 Cap	21 Pis	21 Ari	21 Gem	21 Can	19 Leo	20 Lib	20 Sco	19 Sag	21 Aqu
23 Sag	23 Aqu	23 Aqu	23 Ari	23 Tau	23 Can	23 Leo	21 Vir	23 Sco	23 Sag	21 Cap	23 Pis
25 Cap	25 Pis	25 Pis	25 Tau	25 Gem	25 Leo	25 Vir	24 Lib	25 Sag	25 Cap	24 Aqu	25 Ari
27 Aqu	27 Ari	27 Ari	27 Gem	27 Can	28 Vir	28 Lib	26 Sco	28 Cap	27 Aqu	26 Pis	28 Tau
29 Pis		29 Tau	29 Can	29 Leo	30 Lib	30 Sco	29 Sag	30 Aqu	30 Pis	28 Ari	30 Gem
31 Ari		31 Gem		31 Vir		31 Cap				30 Tau	

JAN	FEB	MAR	APR	MAY	JUN	JUL	AUG	SEP	OCT	NOV	DEC

BORN IN THE YEAR 1999

JAN	FEB	MAR	APR	MAY	JUN	JUL	AUG	SEP	OCT	NOV	DEC
1 Can	1 Vir	1 Vir	2 Sco	2 Sag	3 Aqu	2 Pis	1 Ari	2 Gem	1 Can	1 Vir	1 Lib
3 Leo	4 Lib	3 Lib	4 Sag	4 Cap	5 Pis	5 Ari	3 Tau	4 Can	3 Leo	4 Lib	3 Sco
5 Vir	6 Sco	6 Sco	7 Cap	7 Aqu	8 Ari	7 Tau	5 Gem	6 Leo	5 Vir	6 Sco	6 Sag
7 Lib	9 Sag	8 Sag	9 Aqu	9 Pis	10 Tau	9 Gem	7 Can	8 Vir	8 Lib	9 Sag	8 Cap
10 Sco	11 Cap	11 Cap	12 Pis	11 Ari	12 Gem	11 Can	9 Leo	10 Lib	10 Sco	11 Cap	11 Aqu
12 Sag	14 Aqu	13 Aqu	14 Ari	13 Tau	14 Can	13 Leo	12 Vir	13 Sco	12 Sag	14 Aqu	13 Pis
15 Cap	16 Pis	15 Pis	16 Tau	15 Gem	16 Leo	15 Vir	14 Lib	15 Sag	15 Cap	16 Pis	16 Ari
17 Aqu	18 Ari	17 Ari	18 Gem	17 Can	18 Vir	17 Lib	16 Sco	18 Cap	17 Aqu	18 Ari	18 Tau
19 Pis	20 Tau	19 Tau	20 Can	19 Leo	20 Lib	20 Sco	19 Sag	20 Aqu	20 Pis	21 Tau	20 Gem
22 Ari	21 Gem	22 Gem	22 Leo	21 Vir	23 Sco	22 Sag	21 Cap	22 Pis	22 Ari	23 Gem	22 Can
24 Tau	24 Can	23 Can	24 Vir	24 Lib	25 Sag	25 Cap	24 Aqu	25 Ari	24 Tau	25 Can	24 Leo
26 Gem	26 Leo	26 Leo	27 Lib	26 Sco	28 Cap	27 Aqu	26 Pis	27 Tau	26 Gem	27 Leo	26 Vir
28 Can		28 Vir	29 Sco	29 Sag	30 Aqu	30 Pis	28 Ari	29 Gem	28 Can	29 Vir	28 Lib
30 Leo		30 Lib		31 Cap			30 Tau		30 Leo		31 Sco

BORN IN THE YEAR 2000

JAN	FEB	MAR	APR	MAY	JUN	JUL	AUG	SEP	OCT	NOV	DEC
3 Sag	1 Cap	2 Aqu	1 Pis	3 Tau	1 Gem	2 Leo	1 Vir	2 Sco	1 Sag	3 Aqu	2 Pis
5 Cap	4 Aqu	4 Pis	3 Ari	5 Gem	3 Can	4 Vir	3 Lib	4 Sag	4 Cap	5 Pis	5 Ari
7 Aqu	6 Pis	7 Ari	5 Tau	7 Can	5 Leo	7 Lib	5 Sco	6 Cap	6 Aqu	8 Ari	7 Tau
10 Pis	8 Ari	9 Tau	7 Gem	9 Leo	7 Vir	9 Sco	8 Sag	9 Aqu	9 Pis	10 Tau	9 Gem
12 Ari	11 Tau	11 Gem	9 Can	11 Vir	9 Lib	11 Sag	10 Cap	11 Pis	11 Ari	12 Gem	11 Can
14 Tau	13 Gem	13 Can	11 Leo	13 Lib	12 Sco	14 Cap	13 Aqu	14 Ari	13 Tau	14 Can	13 Leo
16 Gem	15 Can	15 Leo	14 Vir	15 Sco	14 Sag	16 Aqu	15 Pis	16 Tau	16 Gem	16 Leo	15 Vir
18 Can	17 Leo	17 Vir	16 Lib	18 Sag	17 Cap	19 Pis	18 Ari	18 Gem	18 Can	18 Vir	18 Lib
20 Leo	19 Vir	20 Lib	18 Sco	20 Cap	19 Aqu	21 Ari	20 Tau	20 Can	20 Leo	20 Lib	20 Sco
23 Vir	21 Lib	22 Sco	21 Sag	23 Aqu	22 Pis	24 Tau	22 Gem	23 Leo	22 Vir	23 Sco	22 Sag
25 Lib	23 Sco	24 Sag	23 Cap	25 Pis	24 Ari	26 Gem	24 Can	25 Vir	24 Lib	25 Sag	25 Cap
27 Sco	26 Sag	27 Cap	26 Aqu	28 Ari	26 Tau	28 Can	26 Leo	27 Lib	26 Sco	27 Cap	27 Aqu
29 Sag	28 Cap	29 Aqu	28 Pis	30 Tau	28 Gem	30 Leo	28 Vir	29 Sco	29 Sag	30 Aqu	30 Pis
			30 Ari		30 Can		30 Lib		31 Cap		

BORN IN THE YEAR 2001

JAN	FEB	MAR	APR	MAY	JUN	JUL	AUG	SEP	OCT	NOV	DEC
1 Ari	2 Gem	1 Gem	2 Leo	1 Vir	2 Sco	1 Sag	3 Agu	1 Pis	1 Ari	2 Gem	2 Can
4 Tau	4 Can	4 Can	4 Vir	3 Lib	4 Sag	4 Cap	5 Pis	4 Ari	4 Tau	4 Can	4 Leo
6 Gem	6 Leo	6 Leo	6 Lib	6 Sco	7 Cap	6 Aqu	8 Ari	6 Tau	6 Gem	7 Leo	6 Vir
8 Can	8 Vir	8 Vir	8 Sco	8 Sag	9 Aqu	9 Pis	10 Tau	9 Gem	8 Can	9 Vir	8 Lib
10 Leo	10 Lib	10 Lib	10 Sag	10 Cap	11 Pis	11 Ari	12 Gem	11 Can	10 Leo	11 Lib	10 Sco
12 Vir	12 Sco	12 Sco	13 Cap	13 Aqu	14 Ari	14 Tau	15 Can	13 Leo	13 Vir	13 Sco	12 Sag
14 Lib	15 Sag	14 Sag	15 Aqu	15 Pis	16 Tau	16 Gem	17 Leo	15 Vir	15 Lib	15 Sag	15 Cap
16 Sco	17 Cap	16 Cap	18 Pis	18 Ari	19 Gem	18 Can	19 Vir	17 Lib	17 Sco	17 Cap	17 Aqu
18 Sag	20 Agu	19 Aqu	20 Ari	20 Tau	21 Can	21 Leo	21 Lib	19 Sco	19 Sag	20 Aqu	20 Pis
21 Cap	22 Pis	22 Pis	23 Tau	22 Gem	23 Leo	23 Vir	23 Sco	21 Sag	21 Cap	22 Pis	22 Ari
23 Aqu	25 Ari	24 Ari	25 Gem	24 Can	25 Vir	24 Lib	25 Sag	24 Cap	23 Aqu	25 Ari	25 Tau
26 Pis	27 Tau	26 Tau	27 Can	27 Leo	27 Lib	26 Sco	27 Cap	26 Aqu	26 Pis	27 Tau	27 Gem
28 Ari		29 Gem	29 Leo	29 Vir	29 Sco	29 Sag	30 Aqu	29 Pis	28 Ari	30 Gem	29 Can
31 Tau		31 Can		31 Lib		31 Cap			31 Tau		31 Leo

BORN IN THE YEAR 2002

JAN	FEB	MAR	APR	MAY	JUN	JUL	AUG	SEP	OCT	NOV	DEC
2 Vir	1 Lib	2 Sco	1 Sag	2 Aqu	1 Pis	1 Ari	2 Gem	1 Can	1 Leo	1 Lib	1 Sco
4 Lib	3 Sco	4 Sag	3 Cap	5 Pis	4 Ari	4 Tau	5 Can	3 Leo	3 Vir	3 Sco	3 Sag
6 Sco	5 Sag	6 Cap	5 Aqu	7 Ari	6 Tau	6 Gem	7 Leo	5 Vir	5 Lib	5 Sag	5 Cap
9 Sag	7 Cap	9 Aqu	8 Pis	9 Tau	9 Gem	9 Can	9 Vir	7 Lib	7 Sco	7 Cap	7 Aqu
11 Cap	10 Aqu	11 Pis	10 Ari	12 Gem	11 Can	11 Leo	11 Lib	9 Sco	9 Sag	10 Aqu	9 Pis
13 Aqu	12 Pis	14 Ari	13 Tau	15 Can	13 Leo	13 Vir	13 Sco	12 Sag	11 Cap	12 Pis	12 Ari
16 Pis	15 Ari	16 Tau	15 Gem	17 Leo	15 Vir	15 Lib	15 Sag	14 Cap	13 Aqu	15 Ari	14 Tau
18 Ari	17 Tau	19 Gem	18 Can	19 Vir	18 Lib	17 Sco	18 Cap	16 Aqu	16 Pis	17 Tau	17 Gem
21 Tau	20 Gem	21 Can	20 Leo	21 Lib	20 Sco	19 Sag	20 Aqu	19 Pis	18 Ari	20 Gem	19 Can
23 Gem	22 Can	24 Leo	22 Vir	23 Sco	22 Sag	22 Cap	22 Pis	21 Ari	21 Tau	22 Can	22 Leo
26 Can	24 Leo	26 Vir	24 Lib	25 Sag	24 Cap	24 Aqu	25 Ari	24 Tau	23 Gem	24 Leo	24 Vir
28 Leo	26 Vir	28 Lib	26 Sco	28 Cap	26 Aqu	26 Pis	27 Tau	26 Gem	26 Can	27 Vir	26 Lib
30 Vir	28 Lib	30 Sco	28 Sag	30 Aqu	29 Pis	28 Ari	30 Gem	29 Can	28 Leo	29 Lib	28 Sco
			30 Cap			31 Tau			30 Vir		30 Sag

BORN IN THE YEAR 2003

JAN	FEB	MAR	APR	MAY	JUN	JUL	AUG	SEP	OCT	NOV	DEC
1 Cap	2 Pis	1 Pis	3 Tau	2 Gem	1 Can	1 Leo	2 Lib	2 Sag	1 Cap	2 Pis	2 Ari
3 Aqu	5 Ari	4 Ari	5 Gem	5 Can	4 Leo	3 Vir	4 Sco	4 Cap	4 Aqu	5 Ari	4 Tau
6 Pis	7 Tau	6 Tau	8 Can	7 Leo	6 Vir	5 Lib	6 Sag	6 Aqu	6 Pis	7 Tau	7 Gem
8 Ari	10 Gem	9 Gem	10 Leo	10 Vir	8 Lib	7 Sco	8 Cap	9 Pis	8 Ari	10 Gem	9 Can
11 Tau	12 Can	11 Can	12 Vir	12 Lib	10 Sco	10 Sag	10 Aqu	11 Ari	11 Tau	12 Can	12 Leo
13 Gem	14 Leo	14 Leo	14 Lib	14 Sco	12 Sag	12 Cap	12 Pis	13 Tau	13 Gem	15 Leo	14 Vir
16 Can	16 Vir	16 Vir	16 Sco	16 Sag	14 Cap	14 Aqu	15 Ari	16 Gem	16 Can	17 Vir	16 Lib
18 Leo	18 Lib	18 Lib	18 Sag	18 Cap	16 Aqu	16 Pis	17 Tau	18 Can	18 Leo	19 Lib	19 Sco
20 Vir	21 Sco	20 Sco	20 Cap	20 Aqu	19 Pis	18 Ari	20 Gem	21 Leo	21 Vir	21 Sco	21 Sag
22 Lib	23 Sag	22 Sag	23 Aqu	22 Pis	21 Ari	21 Tau	22 Can	23 Vir	23 Lib	23 Sag	23 Cap
24 Sco	25 Cap	24 Cap	25 Pis	25 Ari	23 Tau	23 Gem	24 Leo	25 Lib	25 Sco	25 Cap	25 Aqu
26 Cap	27 Aqu	26 Aqu	27 Ari	27 Tau	26 Gem	26 Can	27 Vir	27 Sco	27 Sag	27 Aqu	27 Pis
29 Cap		29 Pis	30 Tau	30 Gem	28 Can	28 Leo	29 Lib	29 Sag	29 Cap	29 Pis	29 Ari
31 Aqu		31 Ari				30 Vir	31 Sco		31 Aqu		

BORN IN THE YEAR 2004

JAN	FEB	MAR	APR	MAY	JUN	JUL	AUG	SEP	OCT	NOV	DEC
1 Tau	2 Can	3 Leo	1 Vir	1 Lib	2 Sag	1 Cap	1 Pis	2 Tau	2 Gem	1 Can	1 Leo
3 Gem	4 Leo	5 Vir	4 Lib	3 Sco	4 Cap	3 Aqu	4 Ari	5 Gem	5 Can	3 Leo	3 Vir
6 Can	7 Vir	7 Lib	6 Sco	5 Sag	6 Aqu	5 Pis	6 Tau	7 Can	7 Leo	6 Vir	6 Lib
8 Leo	9 Lib	9 Sco	9 Sag	7 Cap	8 Pis	7 Ari	8 Gem	10 Leo	10 Vir	8 Lib	8 Sco
10 Vir	11 Sco	12 Sag	10 Cap	9 Aqu	10 Ari	9 Tau	11 Can	12 Vir	12 Lib	10 Sco	10 Sag
13 Lib	13 Sag	14 Cap	12 Aqu	11 Pis	12 Tau	12 Gem	13 Leo	14 Lib	14 Sco	13 Sag	12 Cap
15 Sco	15 Cap	16 Aqu	14 Pis	14 Ari	15 Gem	15 Can	16 Vir	17 Sco	16 Sag	15 Cap	14 Aqu
17 Sag	17 Aqu	18 Pis	16 Ari	16 Tau	17 Can	17 Leo	18 Lib	19 Sag	18 Cap	17 Aqu	16 Pis
19 Cap	20 Pis	20 Ari	19 Tau	19 Gem	20 Leo	20 Vir	20 Sco	21 Cap	20 Aqu	19 Pis	18 Ari
21 Aqu	22 Ari	23 Tau	21 Gem	21 Can	22 Vir	22 Lib	23 Sag	23 Aqu	23 Pis	21 Ari	21 Tau
23 Pis	24 Tau	25 Gem	24 Can	24 Leo	25 Lib	24 Sco	25 Cap	25 Pis	25 Ari	23 Tau	23 Gem
25 Ari	27 Gem	28 Can	26 Leo	26 Vir	27 Sco	26 Sag	27 Aqu	27 Ari	27 Tau	26 Gem	25 Can
28 Tau	29 Can	30 Leo	29 Vir	28 Lib	29 Sag	28 Cap	29 Pis	30 Tau	29 Gem	28 Can	28 Leo
30 Gem				31 Sco		30 Aqu	31 Ari				31 Vir

BORN IN THE YEAR 2005

JAN	FEB	MAR	APR	MAY	JUN	JUL	AUG	SEP	OCT	NOV	DEC
2 Lib	1 Sco	2 Sag	3 Aqu	2 Pis	3 Tau	2 Gem	1 Can	2 Vir	2 Lib	1 Sco	2 Cap
4 Sco	3 Sag	4 Cap	5 Pis	4 Ari	5 Gem	5 Can	3 Leo	5 Lib	4 Sco	3 Sag	4 Aqu
6 Sag	5 Cap	6 Aqu	7 Ari	6 Tau	7 Can	7 Leo	6 Vir	7 Sco	7 Sag	5 Cap	7 Pis
8 Cap	7 Aqu	8 Pis	9 Tau	9 Gem	10 Leo	10 Vir	8 Lib	9 Sag	9 Cap	7 Aqu	9 Ari
10 Aqu	9 Pis	10 Ari	11 Gem	11 Can	12 Vir	12 Lib	11 Sco	12 Cap	11 Aqu	9 Pis	11 Tau
12 Pis	11 Ari	13 Tau	14 Can	14 Leo	15 Lib	15 Sco	13 Sag	14 Aqu	13 Pis	11 Ari	13 Gem
15 Ari	13 Tau	15 Gem	16 Leo	16 Vir	17 Sco	17 Sag	15 Cap	16 Pis	15 Ari	14 Tau	15 Can
17 Tau	16 Gem	17 Can	19 Vir	18 Lib	19 Sag	19 Cap	17 Aqu	18 Ari	17 Tau	16 Gem	18 Leo
19 Gem	18 Can	20 Leo	21 Lib	21 Sco	21 Cap	21 Aqu	19 Pis	20 Tau	19 Gem	18 Can	20 Vir
22 Can	21 Leo	22 Vir	23 Sco	23 Sag	23 Aqu	23 Pis	21 Ari	22 Gem	22 Can	21 Leo	23 Lib
24 Leo	23 Vir	25 Lib	26 Sag	25 Cap	25 Pis	25 Ari	23 Tau	24 Can	24 Leo	23 Vir	25 Sco
27 Vir	25 Lib	27 Sco	28 Cap	27 Aqu	28 Ari	27 Tau	26 Gem	27 Leo	27 Vir	26 Lib	28 Sag
29 Lib	28 Sco	29 Sag	30 Aqu	29 Pis	30 Tau	30 Gem	28 Can	29 Vir	29 Lib	28 Sco	30 Cap
		31 Cap		31 Ari			31 Leo			30 Sag	

BORN IN THE YEAR 2006

JAN	FEB	MAR	APR	MAY	JUN	JUL	AUG	SEP	OCT	NOV	DEC
1 Aqu	1 Ari	1 Ari	1 Gem	1 Can	2 Vir	2 Lib	1 Sco	2 Cap	1 Aqu	2 Ari	1 Tau
3 Pis	3 Tau	3 Tau	4 Can	3 Leo	5 Lib	5 Sco	3 Sag	4 Aqu	4 Pis	4 Tau	3 Gem
5 Ari	6 Gem	5 Gem	6 Leo	6 Vir	7 Sco	7 Sag	6 Cap	6 Pis	6 Ari	6 Gem	6 Can
7 Tau	8 Can	7 Can	9 Vir	8 Lib	10 Sag	9 Cap	8 Aqu	8 Ari	8 Tau	8 Can	8 Leo
9 Gem	10 Leo	10 Leo	11 Lib	11 Sco	12 Cap	11 Aqu	10 Pis	10 Tau	10 Gem	10 Leo	10 Vir
12 Can	13 Vir	12 Vir	14 Sco	13 Sag	14 Aqu	13 Pis	12 Ari	12 Gem	12 Can	13 Vir	13 Lib
14 Leo	16 Lib	15 Lib	16 Sag	15 Cap	16 Pis	15 Ari	14 Tau	14 Can	14 Leo	15 Lib	15 Sco
17 Vir	18 Sco	17 Sco	18 Cap	18 Aqu	18 Ari	17 Tau	16 Gem	17 Leo	17 Vir	18 Sco	18 Sag
19 Lib	20 Sag	20 Sag	20 Aqu	20 Pis	20 Tau	20 Gem	18 Can	19 Vir	19 Lib	20 Sag	20 Cap
22 Sco	23 Cap	22 Cap	22 Pis	22 Ari	22 Gem	22 Can	21 Leo	22 Lib	22 Sco	23 Cap	22 Aqu
24 Sag	25 Aqu	24 Aqu	25 Ari	24 Tau	25 Can	24 Leo	23 Vir	24 Sco	24 Sag	25 Aqu	24 Pis
26 Cap	27 Pis	26 Pis	27 Tau	26 Gem	27 Leo	27 Vir	26 Lib	27 Sag	26 Cap	27 Pis	27 Ari
28 Aqu		28 Ari	29 Gem	28 Can	29 Vir	29 Lib	28 Sco	29 Cap	29 Aqu	29 Ari	29 Tau
30 Pis		30 Tau		31 Leo			31 Sag		31 Pis		31 Gem

WHAT YOUR MOON SIGN SAYS ABOUT YOU

Now that you know your Moon sign, read on to learn more about your emotional nature and your basic inner needs.

MOON IN ARIES

You have an emotional need to be first. And you want to be first *now*—there's no time to waste. Brimming with enthusiasm and energy, you love to keep busy and find waiting difficult. Remember to open up and talk to those closest to you about your feelings—they can help you to slow down and deal with any difficult emotions as they arise.

MOON IN TAURUS

You love to be surrounded by beautiful possessions and enjoy food and clothes that make you feel good—you have a need for comfort. Familiarity and routine are important to you, and you don't deal well with sudden change. That stubborn streak means you're able to stand up for yourself and protect your own interests, just remember to relax once in a while and try new things.

MOON IN GEMINI

Self-expression is one of your driving forces with this mix. Talking, drawing, writing—you simply have to communicate your feelings. And you love to listen to other peoples' ideas, too. To feed your curious intellect, you've probably got a tower of books and magazines at your bedside. Just don't forget to exercise your body as well as your mind.

MOON IN CANCER

You were born to nurture others—whether that's through baking them a cake or being at the end of the phone when they need your reassuring words. Family is hugely important to you, and you want to feel loved and secure. Being honest about this and accepting your wonderfully sensitive and emotional nature will help you find inner peace.

MOON IN LEO

You have an emotional need to be admired—all you really want is for everyone to love you. Your kind heart and generosity toward your friends and family means you are usually surrounded by others, and the attention you crave is easily won. When things don't go your way, you have a tendency to be dramatic—don't let your pride stop you from asking for help when you need it.

MOON IN VIRGO

You are a gentle soul and appreciate the simple things in life. Helping others in small ways makes you feel needed, secure, and purposeful. A clean and tidy environment is a must, and everything has to be in its proper place. Learning not to fuss when something isn't perfect is a challenge—look for useful ways to keep your practical nature busy and happiness will follow.

MOON IN LIBRA

Close bonds are everything to you—you find strength and stability in your relationships with others. Your need for balance and harmony means you are an excellent peacemaker, skilled at helping people to see and understand another's perspective. Remember to feed your love of beauty with regular trips to art galleries and picturesque places.

MOON IN SCORPIO

Deep and emotionally intense, you need to trust those close to you with your innermost thoughts and desires. All or nothing, you have incredible intuition and can see right to the heart of people. Finding one or two close friends who you can really open up to and be honest with about your feelings is important for your happiness. When this happens, your inner strength is unmatched.

MOON IN SAGITTARIUS

Your need for freedom and space is overwhelming, but when you achieve it, you are bright, breezy, and filled with a zest for life. Always on the lookout for new things to try and people to meet, your energy and enthusiasm lifts the spirits of those around you. Planning is not your strong suit; you prefer to go with the flow and see where it takes you—preferably somewhere fun and interesting!

MOON IN CAPRICORN

Ambitious and practical, you want to work hard and achieve results. You are conscientious and naturally organized, with a clear picture of what you want and how you intend to get there. Remember to take time to kick back and relax—the strong front you present to those around you can hide your more sensitive side. Letting go occasionally isn't a sign of weakness.

MOON IN AQUARIUS

Your desire to be unique and unusual is powerful, and you need the space and freedom to be yourself. Emotionally detached, you are happily independent and have an ability to see the bigger picture. Try not to lose touch with those closest to you—life is full of ups and downs, and friends and family can offer valuable support through tougher times.

MOON IN PISCES

Dreamy and intuitive, your sensitive nature is highly attuned to the feelings of others. Be careful to steer clear of negative people—you're likely to absorb their vibes, and they will bring you down. It's important you learn how to take care of yourself when you feel overwhelmed emotionally. Escaping into a good book or listening to your favorite music can be a great way to reset.

ELEMENTS

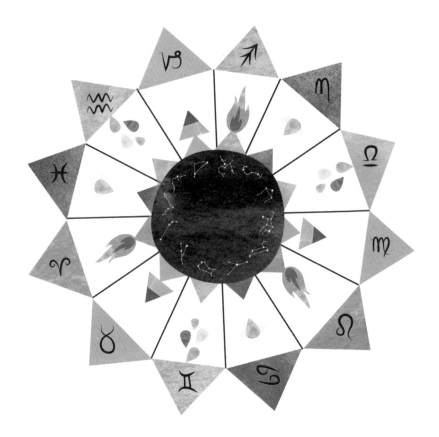

YOUR ELEMENTAL TYPE

Fire, Earth, Air, Water—in ancient times these were thought to contain everything that existed on Earth. Today that's no longer the case, but there's no denying their powerful effect on people's lives. Think of the heat from the Sun, the way earth is used to grow food, the water you consume, the air that you breathe. And like so much in astrology, each element has two sides. You drink water and rain helps plants to grow, but the force of a tsunami can wreak havoc and destruction. You have all four elements within you, but one or more of them will stand out. You could be a single type, or a mix of two or three. Your elemental type says a lot about you and those you interact with. When you meet someone you feel naturally comfortable with, it's often because you are elementally compatible.

IN YOUR ELEMENT

A typical Water sign, Pisces goes with the flow. Emotionally adaptable, you have great powers of empathy. This ability to tap into the feelings of others is your greatest strength and also your biggest weakness. Able to get along with anyone and everyone, you fit into any situation with ease. Just beware of those who would take advantage of your easygoing nature—a little discernment will stop you getting hurt along the way.

 WATER WITH FIRE

Not an ideal mix. Water and Fire can be beautiful together, adventurous and dynamic, but if one is too dominant it can scorch Water's emotions or dampen Fire's energy. When it works, you will bring sensitivity and comfort, while Fire will provide motivation and the courage to act.

 WATER WITH EARTH

Comfortable and secure, you work wonderfully together, each helping the other to reach their potential. Earth is your rock, grounding you emotionally and helping you to get things done, while you refresh and enliven Earth.

 WATER WITH AIR

Air's detached, objective thinking can leave you thirsting for a deeper connection, but Air can also help Water to calm its emotional waves. However, just like a can of fizzy drink, all those bubbles can cause an explosion when shaken or put under pressure.

 WATER WITH WATER

Wonderfully compatible, your relationship is full of feeling, and you love just being together. Sometimes it can be difficult to tell where one ends and the other begins—hold onto your own identity, and don't feel responsible for anyone else's feelings.

THE MISSING PIECE

How dominant Water is within you depends on the influence of the other elements in your chart—ideally all four would be represented. Sometimes a lack of a particular element can cause an imbalance, making you feel rundown or stressed. The best way to counteract this is to tune in to the missing element and reharmonize yourself. Try the simple exercise below to get back in touch with any elements you're missing.

1. First, take a look at the Zodiac signs and their elements.

Fire: Aries, Leo, Sagittarius

Earth: Taurus, Virgo, Capricorn

Air: Gemini, Libra, Aquarius

Water: Cancer, Scorpio, Pisces

2. Now circle Water, as this is the element that represents your Sun sign. You're certain to have some of this element. Then do the same for your Moon sign and your Ascendant, circling the element associated with each.

3. Looking at the list, there should be one or more elements you haven't circled.

Fire—not enough Fire can leave you lacking in energy and motivation. You want to be more assertive and prepared to take the lead.

Earth—a lack of Earth can make you feel disorganized, off-balance, or like you couldn't care less. You might want more routine, structure, or to stay focused.

Air—Air will help you to communicate better, feel more sociable, and lift your spirits. Use it to boost your curiosity and sharpen your wits.

4. Choose the element you would like to tune in to, whichever one you feel might benefit you the most. Then pick one of the ideas from the lists below. If Earth is missing, you could take a picnic to the park and sit on the grass. If it's Fire, you might turn your face to the sun and soak up its warmth. You can use this exercise whenever you feel out of balance.

FIRE

Sunbathe
Toast s'mores
Watch fireworks
Host a barbecue
Meditate on a candle flame
Catch the sunrise
Go stargazing

EARTH

Grow tomatoes
Pick wildflowers
Camp in the garden
Do cartwheels on the grass
Build a sandcastle
Collect stones
Roll down a hill

AIR

Fly a kite
Watch clouds go by
Blow bubbles
Feel the breeze
Play with a balloon
Chase butterflies
Breathe deep

We are
FAMILY

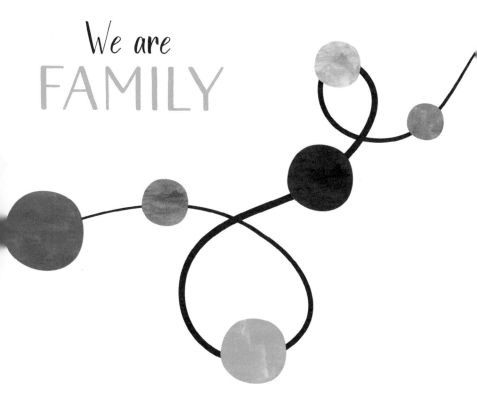

WE'RE ALL IN THIS TOGETHER

When so much in your life is changing, your relationships with your parents can become even more important. If you're lucky, you get along well with yours, but even the most harmonious relationships can come under strain during the teenage years. How can astrology help? It can remind you that parents are people too. They might not get everything right, but hopefully you believe that they have your best interests at heart. Learning more about who they are, why they do things, and how you relate to them can make it easier for all of you to move forward together.

MOTHER MOON

The Moon sign you are born with can tell you a lot about how you see and treat your mother. This is because your Moon sign represents your emotional needs—what you need to feel safe and secure—and these are most often fulfilled by your mother. How you react to her can make a big difference to the way she behaves around you. If you are visibly upset by certain things she does, she is likely to change her behavior the next time around. If you react with happiness and delight, she is more likely to repeat them.

Here's how you see your mother according to your Moon sign . . .

ARIES

You view your mother as strong, honest, and forthright. Sometimes, especially when she doesn't agree with your plans, this can make you feel as though she's taking over. Try not to push back too strongly, and remember she has your interests at heart.

TAURUS

You like to feel your mother is looking after all of your everyday needs and is dependable and reliable. Don't judge her too harshly if she doesn't always live up to your expectations—providing for others is often a careful balancing act, and she is likely doing her best.

GEMINI

Flighty and impulsive, you need your mother to give you the freedom to be yourself and make your own mistakes. Space and independence often have to be earned, though—what could you do to show her you're capable and trustworthy?

CANCER

Your longing for your mother's emotional attention can give you a wonderful bond and connection. However, the slightest hint of rejection from her can wound you deeply. Try not to take her reactions personally—it's okay for her to make choices and have goals that differ from yours.

LEO

You want to enjoy an open, honest relationship with your mother, where both of you say what you mean. Underlying this candor is a need for assurance and acceptance—when you feel vulnerable, be brave and explain to her how you feel.

VIRGO

You are aware of who gives what in your emotional relationship with your mother, and occasionally this can make you feel that she isn't there for you. Viewing her actions as "different" rather than "wrong" will help you to trust she is doing what she thinks is right.

LIBRA

You need your mother to recognize your emotional needs as valid and important. Try not to spend too much time putting others first—your relationship will flourish when you both accept the roles you play.

SCORPIO

You want your mother to respect your emotional boundaries and allow you alone-time when you need it. The trust between you can be intense and unconditional, so much so you may have to remind her to step back occasionally.

SAGITTARIUS

Upbeat and curious, your relationship works best when your mother is inspiring and encouraging, giving you the emotional freedom you need to expand your horizons. It's fine to chase independence, as long as you respect your mother's desire to give you roots.

CAPRICORN

You empathize strongly with your mother's feelings, so when she's struggling, this can make you feel it's your fault. Learn to let go of this guilt—it's unintentional and unhelpful. Instead, recognize how much you need each other's emotional support and encouragement.

AQUARIUS

You're not sure your mother's attempts to guide you are always necessary, and you don't like to burden her with your problems. Asking for help and talking things through might be more useful than you imagine and can bring you closer together at the same time.

PISCES

Your mother's high expectations have made you stronger emotionally, even though there are times when you just want to feel like a child and let her take care of everything. Taking responsibility can be tough; don't be afraid to speak up when you need support.

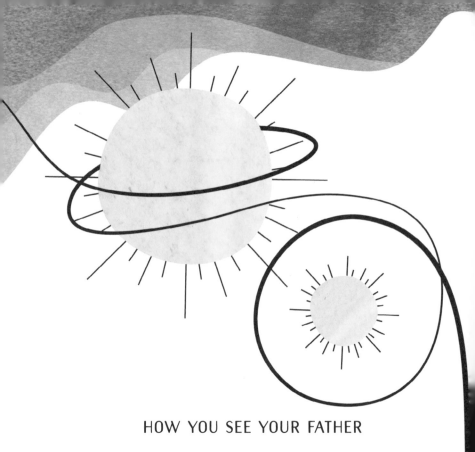

HOW YOU SEE YOUR FATHER

Just as your Moon sign gives you an indication of how you see your mother, or whoever plays that nurturing role in your life, your Sun sign can reveal the way you view your father, or the caregiver who is most involved with discipline. Your relationship with this person is built over time. For girls, it can have a strong bearing on how you view any future romantic relationships, whereas boys will either rebel or identify with these traits.

With Pisces as your Sun sign, you might feel your father is emotionally unavailable. Although you know he loves you very much, you do sometimes get the feeling he's living in his own world. You might even have to remind him when he's agreed to drive you to a friend's house!

Now read on to find out how your father's Sun sign affects your relationship . . .

Your father's Sun sign will play a significant part in how you relate to him, and it can help you to understand why he acts the way he does—however infuriating it may sometimes seem!

ARIES

As a Pisces, beneath the outgoing, bubbly face you show to the world, there is a soft vulnerability that your Aries dad understands. He encourages you to follow your dreams but is likely to shower you with love when things don't go to plan.

TAURUS

Your Piscean creative streak is echoed in Taurus, which is ruled by the planet of Venus and its love of beauty. So, you will while away the hours together, discussing poetry, paintings, and literature. Getting outside could be fun, too.

GEMINI

Your logical Gemini father might find it hard to understand you. That's because as a Water sign you have an emotional view of the world. If you can celebrate your differences, however, you could enjoy a loving and loyal relationship.

CANCER

As Water signs, your relationship can ebb and flow with the tide. But a love of everything creative helps to bond you, so going to the movies or an art gallery together could steer you through choppier times.

LEO

Although you are at opposite ends of the spectrum—Leo can sometimes be self-centered while Pisces puts everyone else first—you balance each other out. It helps that you both have a rich imagination and understand each other's desire for success.

VIRGO

This combination can lead to strong flights of fancy into the realms of imagination. And while it can be a lovely place to be, you'll both need to remember to come back down to earth—sometimes with a bump.

LIBRA

You would both love to shut out the rest of the world because you can't bear its injustices. You have a mature relationship and can talk about serious subjects, but you equally love to hang out on the couch, watching a trashy movie.

SCORPIO

The trust that your Scorpio parent sometimes lacks is buoyed up by your Pisces faith in life. This can create a playful dynamic as you discover new things about the world. Your relationship will keep getting better as you get older.

SAGITTARIUS

You guys always seem to be on the move. That's because you are adaptable signs, able to change in a heartbeat. Your cheerful dad tends to have a warm, friendly hug waiting for you—something your emotional side cherishes.

CAPRICORN

Earth and Water is a winning combination. Your Capricorn dad gives you much-needed boundaries and can help you cope with practical realities, while you make your dad feel strong and capable.

AQUARIUS

Although you may not always see eye-to-eye, you often bond over a desire to help other people. You'll probably be popular with local charities who'll appreciate your fund-raising efforts. Remember to spend time with the rest of your family, too, though.

PISCES

As the symbol of Pisces is two fish, you might feel you have found your other half. Your relationship generally goes swimmingly, unless one of you gets upset. Because your feelings run so deep, you might sometimes lash out emotionally.

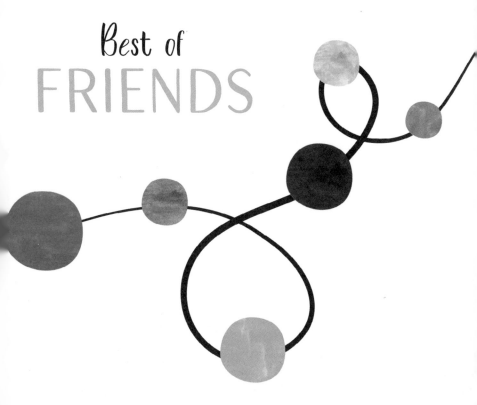

Best of
FRIENDS

FRIENDS FOR LIFE

Friends play an essential role in your happiness. They can help you to move forward when times are tough, see things from a new perspective, and encourage you just to have fun. Every good friend you make has different qualities that will influence you and allow you to make more of your potential. A friend might show you it can be better to hold back when all you want to do is rush in, motivate you to stick with that project right to the end, or inspire you to see an obstacle as a challenge. And astrology can be a great way to highlight those characteristics you're looking for in a friend. It can also tell you more about the type of friend you make for others.

WHAT KIND OF FRIEND ARE YOU?

You're a great listener, you're sympathetic and caring, and you will make time for a friend no matter what. You're the perfect friend to have if someone needs a shoulder to cry on, but you sometimes get too emotionally involved. If there is a problem in a friendship, you are quick to blame yourself, and this will make you insecure. You need a friend who understands you and can reassure you.

Strengths: *Loving, caring, good listener*
Weaknesses: *Sensitive, self-pitying, insecure*
Friendship style: *Supportive, sympathetic, selfless*

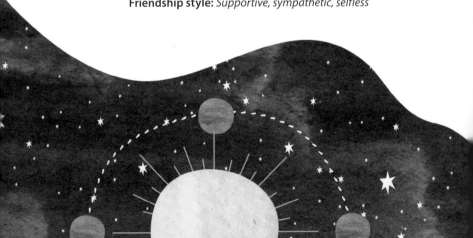

IF YOUR BEST FRIEND IS . . .

ARIES

Aries make friends easily. They're willing to help you achieve your goals, they see the best in you, and they're happy to take risks for you, too. They love to be someone's best friend and can find it difficult to feel second to anyone else. They are always on the lookout for new, super-fun adventures and are happy to take you along for the ride. They have a knack for bringing people from all walks of life together.

Strengths: *Loyal, generous, fun-loving*
Weaknesses: *Insensitive, demanding, petulant*
Friendship style: *Busy, fun, warm*

TAURUS

Considerate and charming, Taurus friends often have a talent for giving good advice. They like to take their time and allow friendships to develop slowly, but once you become close they treat you as a member of their family. As an Earth sign, they are dependable and grounded, and they make wonderful lifelong friends. Bear in mind they can place too much importance on material possessions, even judging others based on their wealth.

Strengths: *Caring, faithful, trustworthy*
Weaknesses: *Judgmental, stubborn, materialistic*
Friendship style: *Helpful, sweet, self-assured*

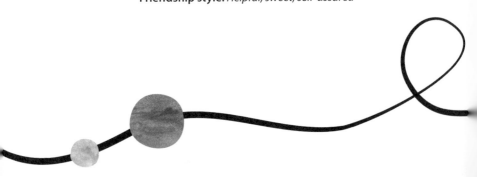

GEMINI

You'll need lots of energy to keep up with a Gemini friend. They love to have fun, do crazy things, and always have a story to tell. They'll make you laugh, but they can sometimes get a little carried away, perhaps exaggerating tales of their adventures in their effort to entertain you. They can be a bit gossipy, but they're not malicious. They're good listeners and will make you feel great, giving you lots of compliments—and always genuine ones, too.

Strengths: *Intelligent, energetic, fearless*
Weaknesses: *Impatient, easily bored, gossipy*
Friendship style: *Good listener, witty, spontaneous*

CANCER

Once you form a close connection with Cancer you have a friend who has your back. They're considerate and like nothing better than to make you feel happy. Watch out though; they're deeply emotional, which means that if you fall out—even over something small—you'll have to work hard to patch things up again.

Strengths: *Loving, caring, intuitive*
Weaknesses: *Unforgiving, anxious, sensitive*
Friendship style: *Warm, affectionate, protective*

LEO

As long as you don't expect too much from a Leo friend, you're in for a treat. Outgoing, confident, and full of energy, they thrive on social occasions and love to be the life and soul of a party, making people laugh and being admired. They're good at bringing people together and are in high demand, so you won't always have them to yourself, but if you can tie them down, you'll have some great quality one-on-one time.

Strengths: *Honest, brave, positive*
Weaknesses: *Arrogant, self-centered, proud*
Friendship style: *Supportive, cheerful, humorous*

VIRGO

With a Virgo by your side you'll always have somewhere to go when times are tough. They'll be there for you, giving you well-thought-out advice and a gentle sympathetic ear. Even when there's not a crisis, they're charming and kind. They like to be organized, so if they make plans, make sure you stick to them. They won't let you down, but they'll expect the same from you in return.

Strengths: *Warm, modest, smart*
Weaknesses: *Shy, serious, overly critical*
Friendship style: *Fixer, good communicator, reliable*

LIBRA

You can rely on your Libra friend to tell you how it is. They have a refreshing honesty, but they also have a diplomatic way of sparing your feelings. They love spending time with you and like nothing better than a chat (especially if they're the one doing the talking!). They can always see both sides, so if there's a disagreement it won't be for long.

Strengths: *Diplomatic, honest, sociable*
Weaknesses: *Indecisive, people pleaser, chatterbox*
Friendship style: *Laid-back, devoted, forgiving*

SCORPIO

It's an honor to be a Scorpio's best friend. They're selective, so they don't always have many, but the friendships they do make will be really special. Once you've cemented your friendship, they'll open their inner circle to you and will want to spend lots of time together. In return, they'll expect 100 percent loyalty and might not take it well if you let them down, so tread carefully.

Strengths: *Passionate, hospitable, perceptive*
Weaknesses: *Guarded, jealous, suspicious*
Friendship style: *Intense, selective, highly loyal*

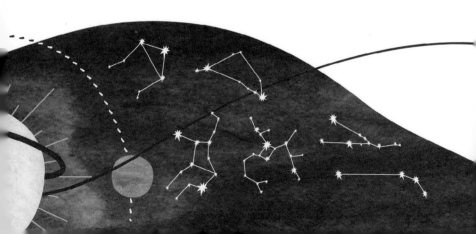

SAGITTARIUS

Sagittarius are low-maintenance friends. Easygoing, positive, and happy-go-lucky, they're up for anything. If you fancy an adventure, give them a call, but don't expect too much of them emotions-wise. Their friendship circle is wide and diverse, so you'll get to meet lots of interesting people, but they are easily bored and can struggle with emotional closeness. On the plus side, they won't put too many demands on you, so give them some space and enjoy the ride.

Strengths: *Adventurous, positive, open-minded*
Weaknesses: *Impatient, insensitive, easily bored*
Friendship style: *Generous, undemanding, never dull*

CAPRICORN

You might have to put in some groundwork, but once you've cracked the seemingly aloof exterior of a Capricorn, you'll have yourself a genuine, warm, loving, and faithful friend. They'll show you complete devotion, through the good times and the bad. They're thoughtful and sensible and will know when to call it a night, but they will often surprise you with their sly sense of humor. They love to make you smile.

Strengths: *Responsible, supportive, faithful*
Weaknesses: *Condescending, standoffish, serious*
Friendship style: *Thoughtful, rational, work hard/play hard*

AQUARIUS

You'll have to share your Aquarius best friend—they'll probably flit in and out of lots of other friendships, too—but rest assured they've got your back and will go to the ends of the earth for you. They'll bring plenty of excitement and fun into your world but they treasure their alone time too, so don't put too many demands on them. They'll never pass judgment on you, no matter what you do.

Strengths: *Tolerant, independent, energetic*
Weaknesses: *Easily bored, rebellious, forgetful*
Friendship style: *Fun, exciting, unpredictable*

Your BIRTHDAY log

List the birthdays of your family and friends and discover their Sun signs

ARIES

March 21–April 20

Passionate, energetic, impulsive

TAURUS

April 21–May 21

Steady, tenacious, trustworthy

....

....

....

....

....

....

....

....

....

....

....

....

....

....

....

....

....

....

....

....

....

....

GEMINI

May 22–June 21

Intelligent, outgoing, witty

CANCER

June 22–July 22

Caring, home-loving, affectionate

LEO

July 23–August 23

Loud, big-hearted, fun

VIRGO

August 24–September 22

Organized, modest, responsible

LIBRA

September 23–October 22

Charming, creative, graceful

SCORPIO

October 23–November 21

Powerful, mysterious, magnetic

SAGITTARIUS

November 22–December 21

Adventurous, optimistic, lucky

CAPRICORN

December 22–January 20

Ambitious, dedicated, serious

AQUARIUS

January 21–February 19

Eccentric, independent, imaginative

PISCES

February 20–March 20

Dreamy, sensitive, compassionate

Lucky in
LOVE

WHY OPPOSITES REALLY DO ATTRACT

The sign opposite your Ascendant (your Rising sign) on your birth chart reveals who you will attract, and who will attract you. Known as your Descendant, it's the constellation that was setting on the Western horizon at the moment and place you were born.

This sign is everything you are not—a kind of mirror image, or two sides of the same coin.

Yet, strangely, you are often drawn to the qualities of this sign over and over again in the people you meet. It's possible that these characteristics are ones you feel you lack yourself, and you sense that the other person can fill in what's missing. Sometimes it really is true that opposites attract!

Ascendant	Descendant
Aries	Libra
Taurus	Scorpio
Gemini	Sagittarius
Cancer	Capricorn
Leo	Aquarius
Virgo	Pisces
Libra	Aries
Scorpio	Taurus
Sagittarius	Gemini
Capricorn	Cancer
Aquarius	Leo
Pisces	Virgo

WHAT DO YOU LOOK FOR?

Once you've matched up your Ascendant with your Descendant from the list on the previous page, you can get to know the qualities that are most likely to attract you. You can use this information whether you're thinking about romance or friendship.

LIBRA DESCENDANT

You're looking for balance and harmony in your relationship, with someone who makes you feel interesting and important. You want to be listened to and value the ability to compromise. Gentleness and sensitivity are the qualities you're searching for.

SCORPIO DESCENDANT

You want an intense, passionate relationship with someone who will welcome you wholeheartedly into their world and want to spend lots of time with you. You are attracted to someone who will take control, but who will also look out for you and protect you.

SAGITTARIUS DESCENDANT

Adventure and fun are what you crave when it comes to love. You want someone open-minded who will accept you for who you are. You need to be given plenty of space to breathe and not be stifled by too many demands.

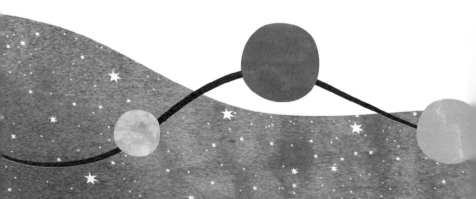

CAPRICORN DESCENDANT

You seek total dedication and devotion from those you love. You're happy to take your time and let a relationship develop naturally, and aren't put off by someone who appears cool or guarded. You like an irreverent sense of humor, too.

AQUARIUS DESCENDANT

You are attracted to someone who is independent and has a full life outside of your relationship, although you want to know that if push comes to shove, they will be right there for you. You like to be kept on your toes.

PISCES DESCENDANT

You're not afraid of a deep relationship with someone who wears their heart on their sleeve. You want to be cared for, emotionally supported, and loved unconditionally. You want to be the center of someone's world.

ARIES DESCENDANT

You like someone to spar with and who lets you have your own way, but is still strong enough to put their foot down when the gravity of the situation demands it. You will need to respect your partner's strength, bravery, and integrity.

TAURUS DESCENDANT

Stability and reliability are high on your list of priorities when it comes to forming relationships. You dislike chaos and are drawn to people who you know won't surprise or disappoint you. Instead you want a partnership that's grounded and safe.

GEMINI DESCENDANT

You're attracted to someone who is spontaneous and fearless, and who can keep you entertained. You're likely to fall for someone who makes you feel super-special and is quick to recognize your achievements and boost your confidence.

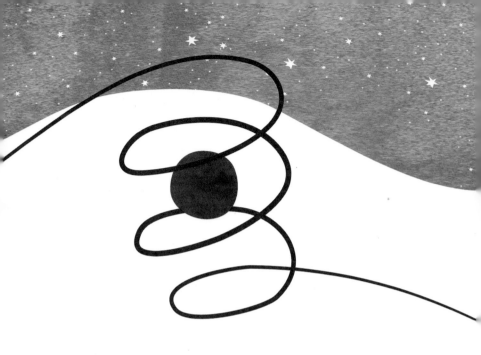

CANCER DESCENDANT

You seek relationships where you're made to feel like one of the family, where your every need and demand is met, particularly emotionally. You want to feel warm and fuzzy and protected by those you love.

LEO DESCENDANT

You're drawn to someone who is strong, confident, and outgoing with a busy social life but who can also give you warmth and passion when required. You're attracted to those who can make you laugh and sweep you off your feet.

VIRGO DESCENDANT

You long for kindness and tenderness in a partnership, along with reliability. You want someone who can bring order into your life and who will think things through in a methodical way. Nothing should be left to chance.

Life at
SCHOOL

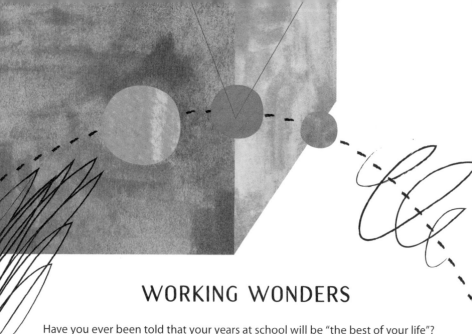

WORKING WONDERS

Have you ever been told that your years at school will be "the best of your life"? Do you think they will be? Why? Many different things will determine how much you enjoy your school days. And there are sure to be ups and downs along the way. But there are a couple of important factors that astrology can help with. The first is determining your skills and strengths, and the second is learning to work well with others. Identifying your natural interests and abilities can help you to develop a sense of purpose, and it's this that is most likely to motivate you to work hard and actually have fun while you do it. To have a sense of purpose, you need to know yourself, and what it is you want from your life. Not what others want for you, or what is expected of you, but what actually makes you come alive.

HIDDEN TALENTS

Not all of your attributes will be immediately obvious. Just because you're a Pisces doesn't necessarily mean you always feel creative, for example. You can think about what a typical Pisces might be good at, but you are unique, and the stars are only a guide. Think about your strengths—both emotional and physical. The examples on the right may strike a chord with you, or you might want to create your own list.

BECAUSE YOU'RE . . . ADAPTABLE

You are resourceful and like variety. You find it easy to do several tasks at once, and you're happy to go ahead with something, even when you don't have a plan.

Maybe you could be a . . .
fisherman, coast guard

BECAUSE YOU'RE . . . CREATIVE

You're full of ideas. You love to work imaginatively and are good at coming up with new ways to do things.

Maybe you could be a . . .
animator, musician, sommelier

BECAUSE YOU'RE . . . CARING

You like to work with other people, especially when their well-being and development is the focus of your work.

Maybe you could be a . . .
scientist, biologist, nutritionist

BECAUSE YOU'RE . . . COOPERATIVE

You are prepared to compromise to get on well with others. You try to keep relationships between others harmonious and help them to see differing viewpoints.

Maybe you could be a . . .
therapist, psychologist, filmmaker

BECAUSE YOU'RE . . . CAUTIOUS

You are a careful thinker and prefer one-on-one communication to large groups. You don't like to take risks, have good judgment and a talent for solving problems.

Maybe you could be a . . .
life coach, counselor, photographer

FAMOUS PISCES PEOPLE

Albert Einstein—*Theoretical physicist*
Daniel Craig—*Actor*
Rihanna—*Singer and songwriter*
Alexander McQueen—*Fashion designer*
Gloria Vanderbilt—*Entrepreneur*
Rainbow Rowell—*Author*
Justin Bieber—*Pop star*

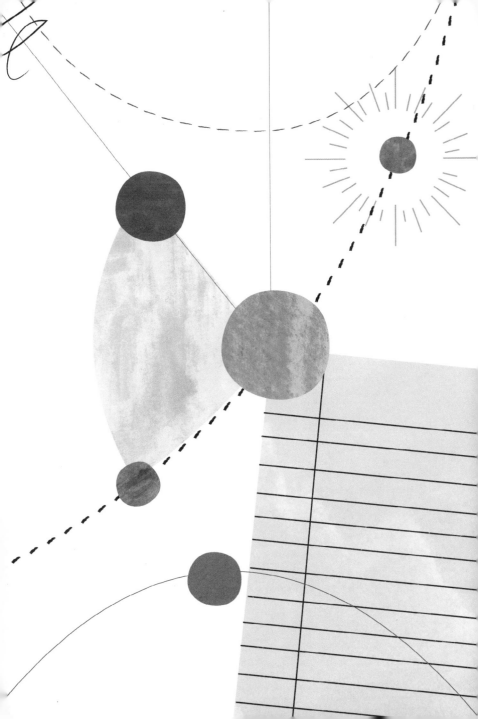

TEAM WORK

Working together with others is essential for almost any career path you choose to follow in later life. School can be competitive, yet working in collaboration with your peers rather than against them builds skills that today's employers are looking for.

Here's how well you work together with . . .

ARIES

Aries can learn a lot from you, so don't be afraid to speak up. These rams could do with a bit of your creativity and imagination to bring an extra dimension to a project. Try not to be sensitive—they can be direct at times—and if you're struggling to keep up, tell them to slow down.

TAURUS

It's night and day with you two, but that often leads to the best collaborations. If anyone can stop you getting carried away with your imagination, it's a well-grounded Taurus, and if the bull gets too bogged down with the gritty detail, you can be relied upon to sprinkle some of your creative magic.

GEMINI

You two work best if the task is creative and the deadline is flexible, allowing your wild imaginations to run free. It might take a while for you to earn each other's trust, but once you click there'll be no stopping you. In the right environment you're the dream team.

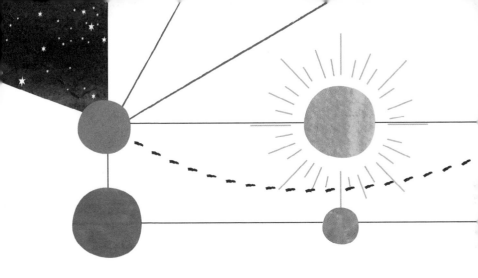

CANCER

There'll be no backstabbing when you two Water signs come together, so you can both relax and go with the flow. Be careful, though, not to let friendship get in the way of work. It's easy to get wrapped up in your emotions, but there are times when you need to stay focused and keep things professional.

LEO

There will need to be a lot of compromise on both sides, for this one to work. The lion will need to learn to bite its tongue, while you'll need to put your emotional needs to one side and be less sensitive. It won't happen overnight, but it will serve you both well in the long run.

VIRGO

You might sit opposite each other on the Zodiac wheel, but provided you both have clearly defined roles, you can be a highly effective team. Combine Virgo's organizational skills with your natural intuition, and the sky's the limit, particularly in customer-service tasks. Just be careful not to tread on each other's toes.

LIBRA

Although you two want the best for each other, there can be an awkwardness at times. While Libra is open and social and loves nothing better than being surrounded by people, you introspective Pisces prefer to keep things close to your chest. A little effort on both sides is required to make this team work.

SCORPIO

You're both dedicated and passionate workers but don't always get the credit you deserve. Neither of you are good at shouting about your work, so your team achievements can get overlooked. Next time, don't be afraid to show off a bit. It's time for your successes to be recognized.

SAGITTARIUS

This team could end up being one-sided unless you're careful. It will be tempting for you to retreat and let Sagittarius take the lead, but the team will get a better outcome with your creative input. Having clearly identified roles and regular meetings will help maintain the balance.

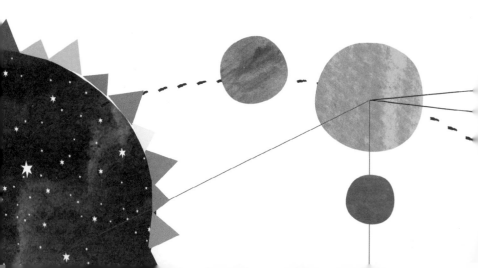

CAPRICORN

Do you follow your head or your heart? That's the conundrum for you two. Find some middle ground, and you could make things happen. After all, you're both capable of seeing someone else's point of view. Go on, try. If you don't, there'll be frustrations on both sides, and you might have to call it a day.

AQUARIUS

You might both feel a little under-appreciated in this pairing, with neither side really understanding the other. Your aspirations are similar but don't quite match up: Aquarius wants the world to be a better place, you want it to be kinder. If you're not careful, this can cause friction at times.

PISCES

You can relax and just be yourself in this partnership. There'll be a mutual respect and understanding that will make working together a joy. Given the right task—the more creative the better—this is the dream team. Just make sure it's more "dream" than "dreamy"!

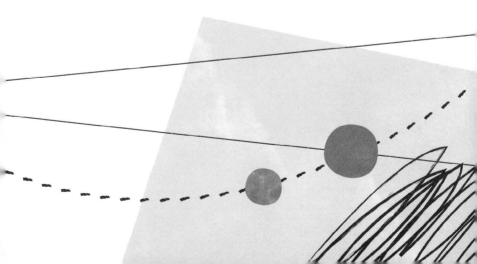

STERLING CHILDREN'S BOOKS
New York

An Imprint of Sterling Publishing Co., Inc.
1166 Avenue of the Americas
New York, NY 10036

© 2019 Guild of Master Craftsman Publications Ltd

ISBN 978-1-4549-3930-6

Distributed in Canada by Sterling Publishing Co., Inc.
c/o Canadian Manda Group, 664 Annette Street
Toronto, Ontario M6S 2C8, Canada

For information about custom editions, special sales, and premium and corporate
purchases, please contact Sterling Special Sales at 800-805-5489
or specialsales@sterlingpublishing.com.

Manufactured in China
Lot #:
2 4 6 8 10 9 7 5 3 1
08/19

sterlingpublishing.com

Design by Jo Chapman
Interior illustrations by Sara Thielker
Cover illustration by Shutterstock